this journal belongs to

· ·

· · · · · · · · · · · ·  · · · · · · · · · · · · ·

what is Sisterhood?

It's not a club or sorority, but a special kind of soul connection—*I can call you sister because you call Him Father.* We don't have to know every aspect of each other's lives; we simply make the decision to recognize ourselves as sisters, because God says that we are.

We believe in sisterhood because we believe in the Church. You see, *ekklesia,* or gathering, is our story. It's how this group got started. A secluded cabin tucked in a tiny camp, miles from a tiny town, served as the backdrop for a fire that sparked in the souls of several sisters. We, along with about 70 other women, had gathered for a retreat. We learned from a phenomenal speaker, worshipped together, shared stories, held hands, ate together, prayed together, and took chances in activities together. As the retreat ended, a cloud of conviction rested over the cabin that several of us bunked in.

> *"This is what the Church looks like—
> and it needs to be shared."*

Fast forward nearly three years to today. The Holy Spirit has been working, and we are now ready to gather women together. It's all about community—finding it, creating it, and sharing it. Online and in-person.

And we are so glad you found your way here.

Sisterhood is

better together.

better together

There is one body and one Spirit, just as you were called to one hope when you were called; one Lord, one faith, one baptism; one God and Father of all, who is over all and through all and in all.

EPHESIANS 4:4-6 (NIV)

Sister, you shine!

YOU RADIATE BEAUTY
INSIDE AND OUT.

Sisterhood

allows you to be you.

you be you

But our bodies have many parts, and God has put each part just where he wants it. How strange a body would be if it had only one part! Yes, there are many parts, but only one body.

1 CORINTHIANS 12:18-20 (NLT)

Sister,
you are His creation.
A unique masterpiece
of great value.
SMILE!

Sisterhood is

being there for one another.

accept

Two are better than one, because they have a good return for their labor: If either of them falls down, one can help the other up. But pity anyone who falls and has no one to help them up.

ECCLESIASTES 4:9-10 (NIV)

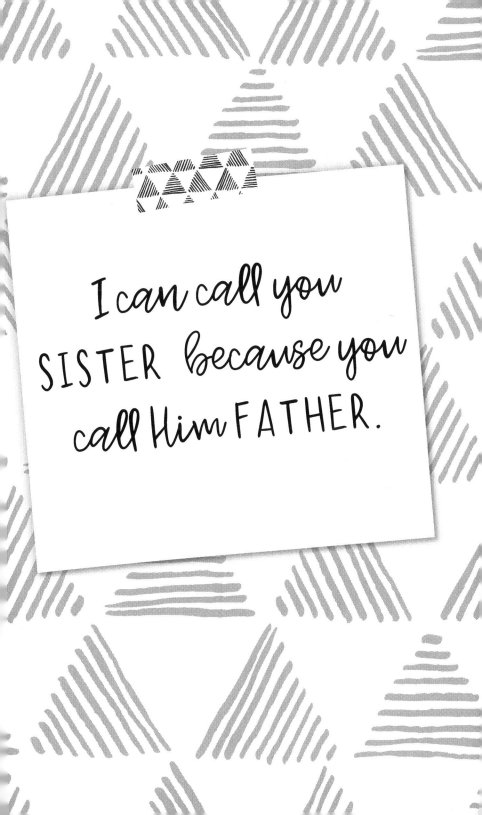

Sisterhood is
knowing you are not alone.

together

May the God who gives endurance and encouragement give you the same attitude of mind toward each other that Christ Jesus had, so that with one mind and one voice you may glorify the God and Father of our Lord Jesus Christ. Accept one another, then, just as Christ accepted you, in order to bring praise to God.

ROMANS 15:5-7 (NIV)

Sisterhood is

loving each other when the chips are down.

no matter what

The heartfelt counsel of a friend
is as sweet as perfume and incense.

PROVERBS 27:9 (NLT)

Sisterhood is

having each other's back.

you're not alone

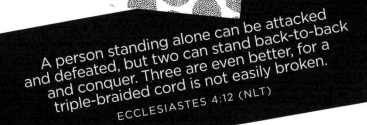

A person standing alone can be attacked and defeated, but two can stand back-to-back and conquer. Three are even better, for a triple-braided cord is not easily broken.

ECCLESIASTES 4:12 (NLT)

Sister, you are chosen and dearly loved.

Sisterhood is
being a safe place.

refuge

When others are happy, be happy with them.
If they are sad, share their sorrow.
ROMANS 12:15 (TLB)

A true friend is always loyal,
and a brother is born to help in time of need.

PROVERBS 17:17 (TLB)

Sisterhood is

taking off the mask.

set free

So God created mankind in his own image, in the image of God he created them; male and female he created them.
GENESIS 1:27 (NIV)

You are the
loveliest of kingdom
workers because your
heart beats in rhythm
with God's.

Sisterhood is
a deep and powerful connection.

Jesus girls

I thank my God every time I remember you.
PHILIPPIANS 1:3 (NIV)

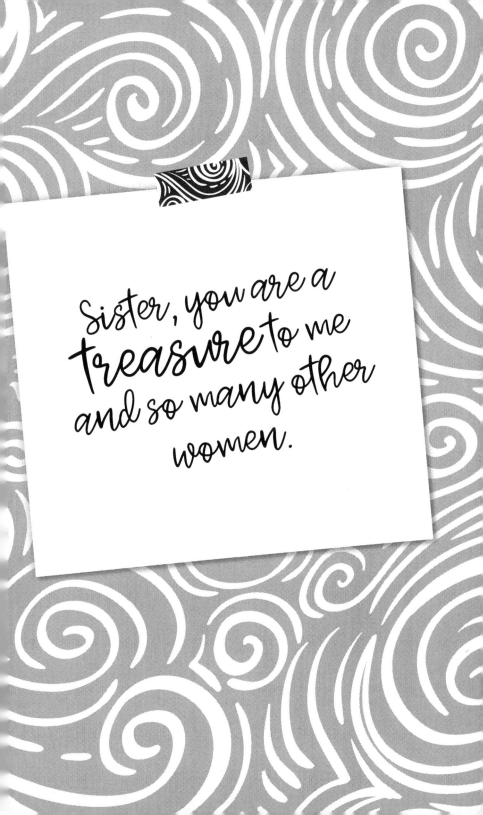

Sisterhood is forgiving when you are hurt.

because we were first forgiven

Be kind and compassionate to one another, forgiving each other, just as in Christ God forgave you.

EPHESIANS 4:32 (NIV)

Sister, when you're feeling overwhelmed, remember... your to-do list is finite and you are an infinite being.

Sisterhood is

never having to go it alone.

walking together

Share each other's burdens,
and in this way obey the law of Christ.
GALATIANS 6:2 (NLT)

GOD HAS GIVEN YOU CARE
OF A GREAT TREASURE.

He loves your family so much and knew you would love them as much.

Sisterhood is

letting our experiences teach us compassion.

understanding

I long to see you so that I may impart to you some
spiritual gift to make you strong—that is, that you and
I may be mutually encouraged by each other's faith.

ROMANS 1:11-12 (NIV)

Sisterhood is all because Christ has come.

we are one

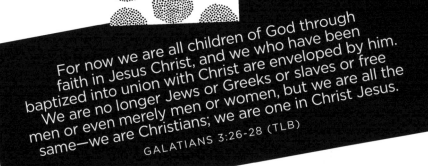

For now we are all children of God through faith in Jesus Christ, and we who have been baptized into union with Christ are enveloped by him. We are no longer Jews or Greeks or slaves or free men or even merely men or women, but we are all the same—we are Christians; we are one in Christ Jesus.

GALATIANS 3:26-28 (TLB)

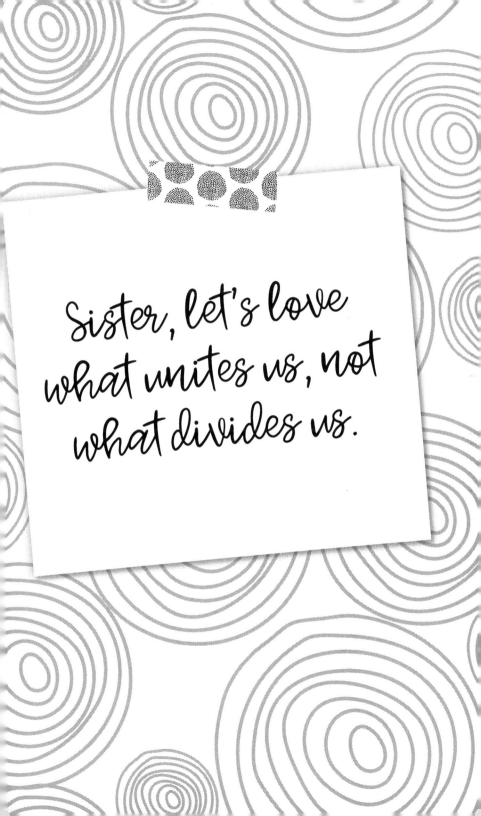

Sisterhood is

cheering each other on.

you go, girl!

Therefore, since we are surrounded by such a great cloud of witnesses, let us throw off everything that hinders and the sin that so easily entangles. And let us run with perseverance the race marked out for us.

HEBREWS 12:1 (NIV)

Sister, Yours is a God-given talent and I admire the way you share it.

Sister, God didn't make you to be like anyone else.

Embrace who you are.

uniquely you

better together

SISTERHOOD JOURNAL

Join the Sisterhood.

· ·

This is not a club or sorority. We are simply a community of women, brought together by our passion to love others as Jesus loves us. We are scattered across the U.S. and have different backgrounds and stories, but we have one very important thing in common: Jesus. He changed us. Sustains us. Frees us. Inspires us. And makes us want to love others.

You don't have to do a thing to be part of this—no membership cards, no initiation activities or qualifications to produce. Just show up. Get involved. Get to know each other. Share your struggles and your joys. Let's do this thing called life together, because although we may not be geographically near each other, our hearts are in the same place, rooted in God, blanketed in prayer, reaching out towards God and one another, sharing our stories to nurture our faith, and joining our lives to grow closer to Jesus in the process. Because life isn't always easy. But God is always good—and we think we are better when we're together.

Follow along on social media or sign up at **sisterhoodministries.com** for updates.

Made in the USA
Columbia, SC
31 August 2019